WHAT BOOKS PRESS

AN IMPRINT OF

THE GLASS TABLE

COLLECTIVE

LOS ANGELES

MIRAGE INDUSTRY

CAROLIE PARKER

LOS ANGELES

Copyright © 2016 by Carolie Parker. All rights reserved. Published in the United States by What Books Press, the imprint of the Glass Table Collective, Los Angeles.

The author would like to thank the editors of the following journals in which these poems first appeared:

Denver Quarterly: "More Enlightenment Ideas," "Untitled (clear)," "The Encyclopedic Collection"
Now Culture: "Found Haiku"

Many thanks to Gail Wronsky, Rod Moore, Annette Leddy and the What Books people for their encouragement and support. I am also grateful to Laura Parker and Katherine Silver for their valuable commentary on the manuscript.

Publisher's Cataloging-In-Publication Data

Names: Parker, Carolie.

Title: Mirage industry / Carolie Parker.

Description: Los Angeles : What Books Press, [2016] | Some of the poems in this book appeared previously in Denver Quarterly and Now Culture.

Identifiers: ISBN 978-0-9962276-5-0

Subjects: LCSH: Women--California--Los Angeles--History--21st century--Poetry. | Los Angeles (Calif.)--Poetry. | American poetry.

Classification: LCC PS3616.A754 M57 2016 | DDC 811/.6--dc23

Cover art: Gronk, *untitled*, acrylic on canvas, 2015
Book design by Ash Goodwin, ashgood.com

What Books Press
363 South Topanga Canyon Boulevard
Topanga, CA 90290

WHATBOOKSPRESS.COM

MIRAGE INDUSTRY

For Peter and Julie.

CONTENTS

Teaching Sappho	13
The Rape of Io, Velazquez	14
Art Studio	15
Untitled (clear)	16
Untitled (transparent)	17
August 18	18
Civil War	19
Pink	20
Language	21
Predynastic	22
Fall Back	23
More Enlightenment Ideas	24
Oedipus	25
Sierra	26
For Sale	27
Tête de Combattant	28
Musée de la Conciergerie: French Revolution	29
Body Art	30
Antigua	31
Untitled (plain)	32
Untitled (lavender)	33
Sphinx	34
Tivoli	35
October	36
XXoo	37

Dance Academy	38
Live Goddess	39
Pseudo Dionysius	40
Survey Course: Colonial to Romantic	41
The Verb Morire	42
Deification	43
Sacred Ball Game	44
Fundação Eugénio de Almeida	45
Histoire de France	46
Gainesville	47
Spinout	48
Essay 2: Tacitus	49
The Encyclopedic Collection	50
Found Haiku	51
Futures	52
Day Job	53
Jade Pendant	54
Three Email Exchanges	55
Mirage Industry	56
Slave for Dreams as Well	57
Domestic and Alien	58
The Current Edition	59
Aeneas and Dido	60

"Entre mi donde y mi cuando, esta mayoría invalida"
—Cesar Vallejo

TEACHING SAPPHO

The missing lines
are replaced with Xs.
Most of the poem is Xs.
A justly famous just one word
to translate, or less, nothing
but the black krater
capable of carrying even breath
or empty
cleared of everything
as we do with
troublesome gardens,
hearts, dams, turbine engines
sending power lines
blindly into the canyon.

THE RAPE OF IO, VELAZQUEZ

These crimes draw
on huge pools of talent.
Zeus sees Io walking.
The Eumenides, called
by the Romans Furiae,
come later.

Can I have her as a present?
asks Hera
Ok, I guess so, Zeus answers
having changed her to a cow.
Argus is guarding.
She traces I O in the dust
(Inachus, her father,
didn't know her).

Velasquez does a painting.
Argus is just a man
struggling to stay awake;
he lacks the armor
of 1000 eyes; Hermes
wears a brass helmet.
Io is a dairy cow.

If not for the cunning
title, I would see a couple
of people and one farm
animal. Maybe that is all
there really was.

ART STUDIO

It would be even
more true more
black, pure black not
that stuff in a bottle
to just give up
to find some other
love in the deep space
of my window
like this guy pulled
along by a red dog
faded to rough patches.
I stand at the clear
glass thinking once
Daniel sat right here
and we talked
in the flat black picture window;
that is how we converse
in my dreams of roller coasters,
water slides, Xibalba.
What would Daniel say
if I wrote him, Daniel,
I think my art has left me
for good. I don't know
my colors anymore,
all nine of them,
lying in their box
like the levels of
Mayan hell.

UNTITLED (CLEAR)

When dreams are
transcribed into language
they are almost pathetic,
birds plucked
by torments, as words
hop along in sentences
trying to explain
what it is to fly, how
to stop the desert from
spreading, whether
a wall of trees could
block it. But enough
of this tangent.
Back to the dreams
where flying was
the original subject.

UNTITLED (TRANSPARENT)

He is going away. Gone.
I get near the bed;
it is still magnetic, given
it is also a body
capable of attraction.
Sleep has nothing
to exaggerate: this acute
sense of deception,
sham birds, poor compensation,
the lack of pity even
in the most tricked out
mechanism (not counting
the haunted garden).

AUGUST 18:

The article
is pretty specific:
explosives
strapped to a bridge,
a poorly
trained militia,
a palace
stripped to the level
of jail,
the Euphrates'
leisurely descent
to desert.

CIVIL WAR

The Death Squad
lost all discretion,
carving big letters
in its victims.
It couldn't even spell
Muerte. How stupid.
It wore a uniform so
people would kill for it,
work dirty, send money.
Still, it never got
the country empty.

PINK

Because it sings
on Spanish radio; pink
because red is just politics; pink
people know what it means
from studying Sappho.
I mention all the hotels
in Lesbos have painted
themselves pink
because it's good business.
Pink scar
across an ordinary face;
pink violation notice
in the usual neighborhood.
Pink, an actual name,
one of my best students;
he really studied. He made it
all the way to Tlon, Uqbar,
Orbis Tertius and came back
with a paper. The excellent
Pink in my extension class
at Addiction Cessation Center.
Pink, who just disappeared.

LANGUAGE

Maybe it was
made for another
history, or I'm
not myself, nobody
known to a country
I wasn't born to
though there are people
and sobriquets
for their children, so why
do we force them
to leave their playthings,
learn an instrument, or stop
the games of pretend?
A thing I love is darkness
on one of its errands,
easy conjugations
like the future,
the generally familiar
in a stranger walking me
through this blindness
until I see even better,
so well it practically
burns the water.

PREDYNASTIC

Mac is
kohl black,
hieroglyphic,
phonetic as the
awl and catfish
reading *Narmer*.
He sits
at the door
very formal
having dragged
home a rat.
In practice, it's
pointless
to scold him,
but *this* is
civilization

FALL BACK

We go into your eyes
for the street performers
and see only a boy walking
Rua da Misericórdia with
a trick dog on his shoulder.

We go into your eyes
and park there; people warm
their hands over a trash fire
near Alto do Lumiar.
This could be my bad, my
patch of weeds, my
ignorance of Portuguese.

We go into your eyes
and stare at River Lethe
as days shorten, step
backward, strip branches
to tinder. You mention
going hot and cold on people;
that must mean this.

We go into your eyes
and reach the end, the limit
a metro station where escalators
drop and drop to the track
at Baixo-Chiado.

MORE ENLIGHTENMENT IDEAS

I like a fine incision,
a field of moving rain,

flat black thunder

considering the body
is hard to inhabit,
considering (coldly)
the faculty of reason favors
whip, leash, collar,
and we don't know
what's down there

a soul, or
just more animal
than I care to handle.

OEDIPUS

The chorus pauses;
the men are wary;
they sense more trouble
to follow with a strophe
an antistrophe
condemned to unity of time
and more starvation.
The aulos measures one animal
in the morning, another
in evening, leading to rough
arguments, a line of questions,
torture coming through
just fine in translation.

SIERRA

How mistaken
To confuse the way
we used to skip
over the hot sand
and race into water
with what we
do now, or to remember
the last detail
of that friendship
studiously ripped to pieces
on a road out
of Angelus Forest
driving back and forth
in fine sutures,
plunging all the way
to desert.

FOR SALE NEAR VENICE

A small island
with original buildings
and piazza jealously guarded
since 1300, but no secret
(160,000 victims of plague
buried in common graves).

They are selling Poveglia
with lines like *fragrant thyme*.
For 700 years it sat empty
growing lavender and roses.
The poor island. In fairness,
plague victims are not
so different from us; finally,
we will die, too, and
nobody will be that happy.

In 1922, a psychiatric
hospital opens, like the past
couldn't travel into certain heads.
Patients worsen. Lobotomies,
electric shock therapies,

solitary isolation.

TÊTE DE COMBATTANT

The head is roughly
modeled, a black
medium, nearly war
with closure
heated, molten, beaten
to hard metal and bolted
to a block of marble.

MUSÉE DE LA CONCIERGERIE: FRENCH REVOLUTION

Mostly head portraits.
Just six jail cells.
Could you pay to get out?
No.
Huge chimneys sandblasted
free of carbon.
Spanish & Italian tour groups
(*dov'è la ghigliottina?*)
followed by trotting school children.
Where is the guillotine?
Oh, they took it away.
So what is here
other than information?
The cavernous building.
This feeling.
The Seine, forcibly
split by an island.

BODY ART

A lot of my students read,
and they're good essentials:
Daniel Alcala burned
with a crown of thorns;
Times New Roman
on Richard's forearm;
no word on Mirna but
a rose bud.

We're still on the Stoics.
We pass now to property.
It's worse to lose
than never own it at all,
Seneca argues. Birds launch
and implode in a tree,
easy to read, a basic shape,

nothing specific, though
I do require it in papers,
writing the same comment:
go back to the text for examples.
A lot of them do it.

All life is bondage,
but the hard can be softened,
the narrow widened,
as Seneca wrote
in indelible letters.

ANTIGUA

Sure, I remember
back five years
then much further
that altitude where
the flame rose and died
having the volcano
almost alive
as the marimba played
I don't remember
what music
worked to the last
note, the lowest thing
beaten by a stick
like walking a street
by myself like
forgetting the simplest
word in a language
then managing
to remember.

UNTITLED (PLAIN)

We argue over the mafia.
I say it's specific to Sicily;
the Ndrangheta is another
story. You say it's
all the same; you see it
in a lot of countries.
What's the difference
between them and the Spanish
fascists? They're different.
No franquista bragged
*I filled a whole graveyard
by myself.* They just
quietly went and did it.

UNTITLED (LAVENDER)

The longest wisteria
tunnel in the world loaded
up on Facebook, followed
by 137,110 Likes.
March, April, May
gone viral.

SPHINX

Night has its slaves,
its chain of sleepers,
building pavilions for
pharaoh. It needs a vehicle,
a stranger's body,
and jumps scene to scene
recruiting dramatis personae.

It favors the blindfold,
the donkey, the sleepwalker
turned three times, *tenderly*,
and drawn to a cliff. Night
is loaded with drug money.

Its most common roles are
Icarus, Oedipus, Caliph—
good practice in flying, in falling,
in riding a camel of smoke
through the desert.

It twists a line, it stumbles
it wants a stunt-double,
one guy I recognize
throwing his voice on tombs,
sensitive and vain
as a playwright, going on two,
going on three, breezing
right through the riddle.

TIVOLI

We go into the church
at Via Due Macelli.
He questions why we need
all this stuff: *fuochi, cuori,
putti*. I would never
ask such a thing. I am not
Italian. I like the flames,
hearts and cupids on the altar.
They are central to tourism;
why raise all these questions?
Let's just go around the church
then down to the gorge
below the tholos temple
and hope for something
better than religion.

OCTOBER

Everything is finished.
It hits the canyon.
Sycamore and eucalyptus
observe the silence.
Here come the children.
If they weren't so resilient,
it would be cruel
to dress them in costumes
and send them door to door
with promises of candy.

xxoo

She was telling me
he is happy
with his 8 cats
and I'm wondering if
it could work for me.
I am probably readier
for cats than ever;
I could start with one
and have it just
bring me the others.

DANCE ACADEMY

Mateo covers up the flame
on his forearms with a dress shirt
and goes around the circle
leading each partner in a spin out.
Then he reels them back in. No casualties.
The instructor says "Try this!"
and does an impossible routine
with the girl in a Burlesque T-shirt.
Mateo rolls up his sleeves,
goes into the circle with burning arms
and does it.

LIVE GODDESS

Ishtar lifts her glorious eyes
and says, "come to me,
Gilgamesh, and be my
bridegroom."
He turns her down. He
doesn't want her demons of
the storm as draft mules.
She left her husband Dumuzi
in Hell, struck Ishallanu and
crippled the Abyssinian roller.
Now he sits in the garden
all day crying kappikappi,
my wing. One student asks
me privately, "why is this
part of our education?"

PSEUDO DIONYSIUS

Night comes in,
right in, walks through
the window like smoke
from the neighbors'
fully loaded grill. I stop
to watch it take the lines,
the birds, the leaves
to a level of perfection
Dionysius the Areopagite
would have praised
from a plane of existence
not this one, but
back to the kitchen,
the darkness, my hand
searching for the switch.
Full electric illumination.

SURVEY COURSE: COLONIAL TO ROMANTIC

She assigned us *Cumandá,*
Don Catrín de la Fachenda
and *María.* "A waste of time,"
said Professor Johnson.
Well if so, it wasn't the sole
thing. There were others.
Zoos with handicapped
animals; learning to play
Ben's flammable piano;
the passato remoto in Italian;
familiar tense in Salvadoran;
classical translation.
Learning the *Odyssey* by heart
and letting it go. Becoming
a Correggio expert
and failing the midterm.
Noli me Tangere,
Et in Arcadio Ego studied,
mastered, vanished
from district curriculum.

THE VERB MORIRE

io muoio
tu muori
lui, lei muore
and more conjugations.
So many.
Loro muoiono is already
too much.
One can always default
to English when things
get this rough, sprung
from random sources,
dangerous and matted
root systems hidden
in rivers of information.
If a vestal virgin let
the fire go out down
in the Roman forum,
she wasn't only killed,
she was tortured.

DEIFICATION

Bronze equestrian statue
of Alexander who
asked to be a god,
was made a god and finished
debased money.

SACRED BALL GAME

We train hard,
driving the body
to indifference,
walking the violent
crosswinds. It takes
all my strength
to feel nothing.
Flower of mine,
remember the loose
thunder, the ninth
trance, how we
followed the dog
to Xibalba.

FUNDAÇÃO EUGÉNIO DE ALMEIDA

The Holy Office of the Inquisition was introduced in Portugal in 1536 and administrated from the Inquisitor's Palace in Evora. Today, the space functions as an arts and cultural forum run by the Eugenio de Almeida Foundation.

Bruce Nauman is in the inquisitor's room/the inquisitor's room is in Bruce Nauman. I don't know which came first, man screaming at woman, or woman screaming at man. Either way, I saw it; it suffices (as video art and performance). The inquisitor's room can take it.

HISTOIRE DE FRANCE

« Mme Pompadour choisit Choiseul
et perd la rive droite du Mississippi »
I read one winter in Paris
« Déjà perdus L'Acadie, La Baie Hudson. »
That is my understanding.
Raw branches; few changes; here, there
a flower. Then winter finishes
like whole nations snapped off
at the river, French and Indian names,
painful serration and now
slightly cooler weather as if
someone slammed the balance
so nothing weighs.
One thing passes to another
leaving the same grey birds as ever
and sending a letter postmarked
Louisiana. You write one last time.
That is normal, losing seasons,
countries, people.

GAINESVILLE

A huge alligator suns itself
in the swamp, filling a
pause in conversation.

We don't talk
about the collapsible beds
at county hospital, how they ride
the halls as you lie there,
or speak of death as a thing
place or person, nor
do we get out our poems
and ask, What do you think
about the ending?

SPINOUT

I touched him.
It couldn't
be turned off
like a radio singing
que tonto que necio
que somos tu y yo.
Just because I'm alive
doesn't mean I had to
dance with him,
but I did,
cumbia, meringue,
I thought *how easy.*
Well, it wasn't.

ESSAY 2: TACITUS
(SUPPORT YOUR POINTS WITH SPECIFICS)

What is a "specific"?
Druid witch is a specific.
Women *like furies*; women
brandishing torches,
consulting gods via
human entrails are specifics.

Are we done with the
Uprising in Britain?
Do you want more?
One student does:
This weird spectacle awed
the Roman soldiers into a
state of paralysis.

This is what Edgar writes:
The Roman soldiers
just have to suck it up.

THE ENCYCLOPEDIC COLLECTION

It is hard to sum up
the essential in this format.
When a morning passes
through me, it is final;
birds ride to extinction
with it. Before you know
it is noon, evening, fin
in Sphinx's riddle.

FOUND HAIKU

Italian woman
in right to die
debate dies

FUTURES

There is no way to tell which palm reader is best without trying each. One speaks with a Southern accent. He holds my left wrist; the pulse is a little fast. Everything's fine he says with an air of fatigue. I ask him about the lines on my palm. He looks into it like he'd forgotten. *Generally, when you cross one degree of longitude, another will appear.* Well Kaiser Wellness Program could have told me that. The sobering standardization creeps along Venice Boardwalk until each stand advertising *Psychic* is decorated with moons, stars and rings of Saturn.

DAY JOB

I help Jean-Yves prepare the fundraiser. I'm hungry. *Je crève de faim.* He asks where I learned that phrase (don't use it). Uh, at a boat party. We dressed up as pirates and flew the skull and crossbones. He listens in silence. We unfold all the flimsy tables and float white cloths over them; the room is ghostly formal. He announces to anyone in earshot "Elle a passé le weekend avec des marins."

PENDANT

We are studying the Americas chapter; I point the green laser at Baby Jaguar. He is probably a better animal than man. How do I know this? The houses of Xibalba. There's a House of Hurricanes, a House of Earthquakes, a House of Monkeys and they're all human. That is our nature, to force coral red into jade incisions; to add five terrifying nameless days to perfectly good ones.

THREE EMAIL EXCHANGES

Mireya: Will we have tea? Me: No, just the usual junk food. Mireya: Oh, I'm sorry the autocorrect changed it. I wanted to know, will we have a test?

· · · · · · · ·

Johnny: Did I pass the test? Me: No. Where have you been? Johnny: I got in a motorcycle accident. Me: Are you Ok? Those things are so dangerous. Btw, it was the ldtd, so I dropped you. Do you want to add back on? Johnny: Can I pass? Me: the best you could get is a D. Johnny: What do I have to do for the D?

· · · · · · · ·

Me: Brent and Antonia, I'm asking you both to please get along. Brent: I know but I tried to be nice to Antonia and shared my notes and can't help that I'm always coughing. Me: Ok, I know you're trying. Brent: I'm sending you a jpg of the Super Moon over Cape Sounion.

MIRAGE INDUSTRY

They film a sequel to Scream 2 at the neighbor's mansion. The night is calm; we hear the screams filmed over and over. The actors and actresses must be exhausted. I hope they don't end badly, like casualties of war in Goya y Lucientes. The next night, they scream even louder. An agent goes door to door giving people another hundred dollars in cash. That buys our silence.

. . . .

They're shooting World War Z at the neighbor's. The street is packed with trailers. One of them, called the honey wagon, has parked in front of our house. For that we get a hundred dollars more. A sweet deal. At lunch and dinner, zombies break out of their haunts. They're rather friendly. Late at night, they move through my dreams in packs insisting it's all just an act.

SLAVE FOR DREAMS AS WELL

It is hot; it will get worse.
We cycle into a trend of drought
rough as *The Book of Samuel*. Everywhere
the Ark of the Covenant travels,
a plague of sores and rat population follows.
The Hebrews' enemies send it back.
They cast five rats and five hemorrhoids in gold
and get the whole thing on the road.
If it heads to Beth-shemesh, that
is a bad sign.

DOMESTIC AND ALIEN

Some words are so close,
they go right down to the root
language. Anglo-Saxon
without the balancing aegis
of Latin. Fall, night—worse
I feel them
drop leaves all over the grass
until it is silent; through the air,
in the streets, there is nothing.
Trees and branches wander
with no awareness they are naked;
it goes far back
as conversion, imported religions,
stars laid over with
mythological assurance.

THE CURRENT EDITION

You can get a former edition of *Gardner's Art Through the Ages* much cheaper on line. The 10th edition is only a penny. Now that the author is dead, the book is ghostwritten by committee. Ghost writers tread more gently than a live author. They offend neither the dead nor the living. Helen Gardner says that Jean Goujon's *Three Graces* would be just a lame copy of the mannerist norm if the nymphs didn't have a certain *French chic*. The new edition simply calls them four beautiful maidens. Helen Gardner says the *Flavian Woman* has a *crooked neck*; the ghost writers revise that to *elegant* and *swanlike*. When Bernini is refused a commission in Paris, he returns to Italy *in high indignation*. This last part is still in. If you want something less hurtful, pay full price for the 15th Edition.

AENEAS AND DIDO

We skip the shipwreck.

We go straight to Hades.
The scene where
Sibyl leads Aeneas
to a shady Nowhere. No,
we have not been alive
long enough to really know;
to say this is possible
impossible (sun pours
into the classroom).
Aeneas and Dido
are down there,
she backing into the dense
underworld forest, he
dumbly alive and
deaf to her silence.

CAROLIE PARKER has a background in visual arts and foreign languages. She was recently a MacDowell Fellow in poetry and a Visiting Artist at the American Academy in Rome. Her work has come out in *The Denver Quarterly*, *Now Culture*, *River Styx* and *Trickhouse*. She teaches humanities and art history at LA Trade Tech College in Central Los Angeles.

LOS ANGELES

TITLES FROM
WHAT BOOKS PRESS

POETRY

Molly Bendall & Gail Wronsky, *Bling & Fringe (The L.A. Poems)*

Laurie Blauner, *It Looks Worse Than I Am*

Kevin Cantwell, *One of Those Russian Novels*

Ramón García, *Other Countries*

Karen Kevorkian, *Lizard Dream*

Holaday Mason & Sarah Maclay, *The "She" Series: A Venice Correspondence*

Carolie Parker, *Mirage Industry*

Patty Seyburn, *Perfecta*

Judith Taylor, *Sex Libris*

Lynne Thompson, *Start with a Small Guitar*

Gail Wronsky, *So Quick Bright Things*
BILINGUAL, SPANISH TRANSLATED BY ALICIA PARTNOY

ART

Gronk, *A Giant Claw*
BILINGUAL, SPANISH

Chuck Rosenthal, Gail Wronsky & Gronk,
Tomorrow You'll Be One of Us: Sci Fi Poems

PROSE

Rebbecca Brown, *They Become Her*

François Camoin, *April, May, and So On*

A.W. DeAnnuntis, *Master Siger's Dream*

A.W. DeAnnuntis, *The Final Death of Rock and Roll and Other Stories*

A.W. DeAnnuntis, *The Mermaid at the Americana Arms Motel*

A.W. DeAnnuntis, *The Mysterious Islands and Other Stories*

Katharine Haake, *The Origin of Stars and Other Stories*

Katharine Haake, *The Time of Quarantine*

Mona Houghton, *Frottage & Even As We Speak: Two Novellas*

Rich Ives, *The Balloon Containing the Water Containing the Narrative Begins Leaking*

Rod Val Moore, *Brittle Star*

Annette Leddy, *Earth Still*

Chuck Rosenthal, *Are We Not There Yet? Travels in Nepal, North India, and Bhutan*

Chuck Rosenthal, *Coyote O'Donohughe's History of Texas*

Chuck Rosenthal, *West of Eden: A Life in 21st Century Los Angeles*

Chuck Rosenthal & Gail Wronsky, *The Shortest Fairwells are the Best*

What Books Press books may be ordered from:
SPDBOOKS.ORG | ORDERS@SPDBOOKS.ORG | (800) 869 7553 | AMAZON.COM

Visit our website at
WHATBOOKSPRESS.COM

www.ingramcontent.com/pod-product-compliance
Lightning Source LLC
Chambersburg PA
CBHW020625300426
44113CB00007B/782